Our Echo of Sudden Mercy

Our Echo of Sudden Mercy

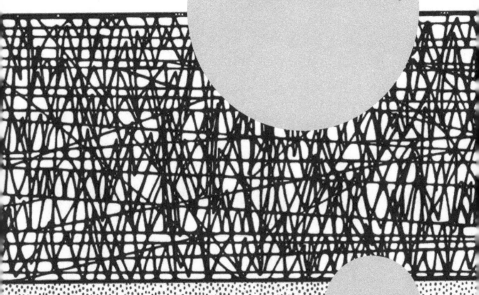

Hari Alluri

NEXT
PAGE

Published by
Next Page Press
San Antonio, Texas
www.nextpage-press.com
© 2022 Hari Alluri. All rights reserved.

ISBN: 978-1-7366721-2-9

Book team:
Laura Van Prooyen
Cathlin Noonan
Faisal Mohyuddin, Cover Image
Julay, Cover Design
Amber Morena, Book Design

Dedicated to the memory of Eric Cardeño

—Wundrkut Forever—

Contents

Our Echo of Sudden Mercy

they have never left, they who 'storytold' before us,
they who are under our skin.

—*Merlinda Bobis*

Situation Card: "an inversion of the gaze"

I rub my eyes at the wake-up song, reach across my journal to quell the alarm. And now my phone is in my hand and my dreams begin to fade. The online world floods in, and I'm not ready, and I keep scrolling.

The easiest days begin when I've cleaned the stovetop espresso maker the night before.

Most mornings the coffee grounds decorate the counter, spill, bother my bare feet. And not just mine.

When I take too long to get up to my first smoke, I'm grumpy before I do.

In another version of the story, my notebooks
on the stove, the only things that burn.

You never know when the fire will ask you to be its home.

I ask one of my demons: hold me with the precipice of you, gathered under the constellation of migration. Make the bonfire a laughing thing, like the ritual distance that marks each step.

Wrote this years ago, and it returned:

Foundation sounds like clove-chop in rhythm, the kitchen—
before the richness of stew fills the room,
it stays on my fingers like lingering grooves.
Kiss fear eyes open, Foundation say, *move*,
sweet ash of flowers surrounding a tomb.

In another version of the story, I start to miss those of you
I've only met on Zoom. Refuse to admit
mumbling, "I love you," after we hang up. I would ask
the Deity of Lost Things to disappear this mess, but I'm
pretty sure that's the opposite of why They come around.

Bless the overflow as I tie the kitchen garbage bag. Bless the Trader Joe's paper one from the last time I crossed south that helps me carry compost bags: freezer to alley bins. Bless its paper handle that finally breaks, more than a year now of it not breaking.

Anger because the coffee grounds,
their desire to spread. The haunch of me
at them. Anger because I'm scared
to say, "I'm drowning"—bless it. Say it:
I'm drowning. Say it to mean
drowning is a form of being held.

☉

Obstacle Card: "foundations are being shaken"

Beneath the earth the earth
is always rumbling.

And here, a little helplessness to hold like a newborn child—
it's not the child who's helpless it's the holding.

Please, don't appropriate
this error into the good small
moments of your days—*we need more
betrayal if we want to keep forgiving*—not if you believe
that language is a spell.

Blessed are those
who ghosts and demons
flock towards. And every time, ingat,
my loves. My loves: Ingat.

If you ever get to watch the eggs fall as you rush them
out the fridge, crack on the lip left by its open door, spill
there and onto the linoleum as they tumble; if you towel
those eggs up, sob-sobbing the whole time, "I can't do this, I
can't," hand and knees to floor, "I can't," pour the surviving
yolks, from the somehow upright carton into the already-
warmed-up frying pan, no need to panic:
there will be other chances not to quite pull through.

Is it possible that countries do not have a body the same way
my knees my hips my spine my lips don't have a country?

It's true: some days will sorrow more than other days,
and the lightest drizzle mocks us by refusing to downpour.

That must be part of it, yes? The gravity we need?
Strong enough to pull down rain, weak enough to let it rise,
kind, no maybe soft, or dare I say it generous
enough we aren't pummeled always by the falling.

In a feathered version of the story, we offer
thirst, we drink it well. And no-one is dehydrated
in the 72-hour cuddle puddle reunion still to come,
the one not all of us imagine quite the same.

We already know who harms the water most. And how
wide is your who? Ask, moving your body, in tune
with the way you ask: in whose bodies lives the water
I'm here to speak more softly to? To listen towards?

There's no lashing quite like the one that lashes to stay
disconnected. Unlike this horizon in a giant tree
whose leaves—every and each—turns, capsizes
into a bat. Descending to the lake before taking up the sky.

In a less-winged version, on the rooftop
balcony of my fury at myself, there's a poem
about my grandmothers I never write and no other
story I tell after that.

Lola, Dadi, Nana, Bai. Orasyon, foundation.

What towers over us: a body of stories, shard-style
and kaleidoscope, towering over etch-a-sketch arcs, partial,
shaken up. Refusing to fall away.

You rarely know when the consequence of your masks will be
another's suffering, but ooh, you know it will.

When my lover's daughter's tween-on-phone squeal breaks all
upper registers—into soundlessness—it means a word for joy
poets haven't invented yet.

And yet, I hear it and remind her to do her dishes.

Glancing in while watering our patio garden-try one day,
I see her wiping the sole of one affected foot
on top of the smoother one, to lose the coffee grounds.

It's the smudges on the window that hold onto the light.

My people say, "Isang bangka."
It also means we have work to do.

I'm thinking of a boulder on top of a hill just out of view from
the hallway before migration I was trying to look away from, a
boulder the shape of a boat that balances and could be tipping,
could many times have tipped.

It was the yogi teacher I thought I looked up to who lifted my
friend at the wall. The government who would hear the name
of the child and say the teacher had to.

In a city version of that story, the rooftops
know it's not the kites that fight, but the shatter-
glass the children rub into our strings
beneath. The way we hold them
tethered to ourselves, the part of us that cuts

(this is what I thought the word ganja meant. I didn't
think of river).

We have always been the consequence of stories.

I leave out the version where Amangaolay is a creator god.
Peace be upon the surrenders I evade. I want to wake up to
the sound of my demons snoring as they dream.

Something like this:

the drum-line dropping out of a hip-hop track
and the deejay scratches crow-wings into city sky at dusk;
as saplings dig their roots into the carcass of a fallen tree,
Mahal caresses the inner part of my upper arm,
calling that arm that's worked so much a thing that's soft.

☉

Response Card: "when all seems too much"

In another version of the story, I'm a jungle and migration
is the undergrowth of me.
I say mobilize and it becomes a kind of prayer.

What I don't know about what will happen next could fill
the amphitheatre of every valley my feet have touched
with a symphony of instruments I never learned to play.

The homie, from a region I am almost from, his favourite songs
offer incompletion: they leave space for him   to be
with his longing.

I say belong and I tell you I am
afraid community is impossible. I put on a ritual
mask and speak
into the mirror. I say mask and I mean to unmask my demons.

I think if I wanted something for this now, it would be a form of radical trust I fear I can't afford. And yet, we sit in circle with each other, via all these screens, write something old–new into the world and share it like we trust.

We search and every moment we don't find is a moment of us searching, widening the reach of the one we search for, the way he'd stick his arm out to make room for a hug.

Know that we did everything we could
And if asked to find the strength
To do more,—we would.

Already the previous story has visited me twice since.
It means I am one of those lucky ones it hasn't made a home.

When we Kut through all else sometimes all we're left with is
Wundr.

I think this might be history's bass line, a myco–ether,
the forest fires that we're from, teeming now as jungle—

may the plant who needs the canopy's shade find a branch
above, may the one who stretches up find itself a clearing. You
and the Deity of What's Lost, may you be less overworked.

In another version, I
kapwa to so many mothers' griefs
and my mother's as well.

I iron her blouses while I whisper names,
and she tells me her stories.

There is yet another *we* who you can recognize,
by the precipice in a glinting-
shake that never leaves our jaws.

I say relinquish, the Deity of Lost Things is taking
this English. When I say nourish with a flourish I mean
the Dream, the circles of us, bahala na: Kapwa.

The stories of those we love they never tell with their mouths—
listen. The ones that find us when needing their stories, find us
by way of other mouths after their hands have left.

Echo: all those times you pulled a record
back to let it go, something happens to the molecules in
the air and in my body.

There are waters who will not approach
for anything less than song.

I have to tell myself this story now, as if I trust
the version of me in it will find a way to be:

There's tears in our eyes just to say hello. How beautiful
the etchings of the world are on our bones,
on our work-torn muscles and the creases beside our eyes.

The languages they hide, incomplete, tell you only this:

we have un-walled this whole city with the joy of our ghosts,
burning down the kingdom where our suffering was the sun.

⊙

Notes and Acknowledgments

After Faisal Mohyuddin's "Ghazal for the Diaspora"
After Gémino H. Abad, Chris Abani, Phanuel Antwi, Rick
Barot, Kay Ulanday Barrett, Tarfia Faizullah, Joy Harjo, Jayson
Krawchuk, Jason Magabo Perez, Justin Phillip Reed, Barbara
Jane Reyes, Dylan Robinson, Shaunga Tagore. Prompted,
guided, held by Faria Ali, Miguel Angel Angeles, Neela Baner-
jee, Raychelle Heath, Arthur Kayzakian, David Maduli, Aurora
Masum-Javed, Khari Wendell McClelland, Cecily Nicholson,
Cynthia Dewi Oka, Seema Reza, Laura Van Prooyen.

With section titles quoted from "The Foreigner" (Konrad
Ng and Simi Kang, *Asian American Tarot*—Mimi Khúc and
Lawrence-Minh Bùi Davis, eds.), "Imperyalista—The Tower"
(Jana Lynne Umipig, *Kapwa Tarot*), "Relief—End Strife"
(Marcella Kroll, *Sacred Symbols Oracle*). With quotations from
Carlo Sayo and Sol Diana, respectively.

This project was originally concocted as part of *The
Essentials*, presented by The Cultch and Soft Cedar, with
thanks to Khari Wendell McClelland and Meghan Robinson.
I acknowledge the support of the Canada Council for the Arts.
This work wouldn't be without Kapwa: BIPOC Writing Party,
The Capilano Review, Cinder Block, Community Building Art
Works, The Digital Sala, A Gatheration, Hilot Academy of

Binabaylan, Massy Books, Next Page Press, Sampaguita Press, Voices of Color Crew, The World We Want.

Love to everyone—near and far, directly and indirectly—involved in the search for and ongoing honouring of Eric. Respect and love to the Skratcher crew and the TableTutors fam.

To Niki and Kaya; to the Cardeño and Silva families; to Team Danger; to Popsi. For Adalao; for Encarnación; for Eralin; for Hannah; for Jhansi; for Kat; for Leila; for Maria; for Neelam; for Nenix; for Olivia; for Paul; for Qayyum; for Reesie; for Rehan; for Jos and Carmen; for Chris and Dags. And to all who've lost, for those you hold.

For who holds now and next: Aaron, Aikulola, Ali, Alva, Amélie, Anaiya, Apollo, Aria, Arvin, Avnika, Bonnie, Briggs, Cal, Camilo, Cara, Ceire, Cynthia, Devon, Eli, Eva, Finn, Honey Rose, Iliana, Imaan, Isaac, Isana, Isley, Isobel, Jovan, Kabir, Kai, Kailash, Kalani, Kalayaan, Kanoa, Keiris, Kiera, Kyle, Leila, Leo, Luke, Luna, Malia, Maren, Maya, Mia, Mya, Naviya, Nima, Norrin, Omar, Paul, Phoenix, Prince, Raiden, Ria, Rielle, Rohan, Roman, Sasha, Sienna, Silver, Siyana, Sunum, Tanya, Witton, Xyriez, Yvan, Zayan, Zuleihka, and beyond—

With extra special thanks to FeRinaKrish, for this life

And to Julay and Tala, for this home: mahal kita.

All salamat everything.

—Wundrkut Forever—

About the Author

Erik Haensel

Hari Alluri (he/him/siya) is a migrant poet of Filipinx and South Asian descent living and writing on unceded Coast Salish Territories of the Musqueam, Squamish, and Tsleil-Waututh peoples and Kwantlen, Katzie, Kwikwitlem lands of Hənq̓əmin̓əm̓ speaking peoples. He is author of *The Flayed City* (Kaya), *Carving Ashes* (CiCAC/Thompson Rivers), and chapbook *The Promise of Rust* (Mouthfeel). Writer-director of *Pasalubong: Gifts from the Journey* (NFB/ONF), co-editor of *We Were Not Alone* (Community Building Art Works) and co-founding editor at Locked Horn Press, siya has received grants, fellowships, and residencies from the BC Arts Council, Canada Council for the Arts, *The Capilano Review*, Deer Lake, Martha's Vineyard Institute of Creative Writing, VONA/Voices, and others. His work appears through these venues and elsewhere: *1508, AALR, Apogee, Four Way Review, Marías at Sampaguitas, Poetry, PRISM International, Witness,* and—via *Split This Rock—Best of the Net 2022.*

CPSIA information can be obtained
at www.ICGtesting.com
Printed in the USA
LVHW032113181022
731001LV00003B/153